Aural Training in Practice

ABRSM Grades 4 & 5

John Holmes Chief Examiner
Nigel Scaife Syllabus Director

ABRSM

The authors would particularly like to thank Timothy Barratt and Julian Hellaby for contributing ideas and music examples to *Aural Training in Practice*; they would also like to thank Alan Bullard, Stephen Ellis, Ruth Gerald, Stephen Pinnock, David Ponsford, Michael Rose and Edward Warren for their help in preparing this series.

Please note that for the purposes of this book some of the music extracts have been freely adapted.

First published in 2011 by ABRSM (Publishing) Ltd, a wholly owned subsidiary of ABRSM, 24 Portland Place, London W1B 1LU, United Kingdom

© 2011 by The Associated Board of the Royal Schools of Music

ISBN 978 1 84849 246 2

AB 3564

Cover and text design by Vermillion
Music origination by Julia Bovee and Katie Johnston
Text origination by Julia Bovee
Printed in England by Caligraving Ltd, Thetford, Norfolk

Recording credits:
Played and presented by Juliet Barwell
Recorded in July 2010, November 2010 and January 2011 at Red Gables Studio, Greenford
Produced by Sebastian Forbes
Balance Engineering by Ken Blair
Audio Editing by Ken Blair
A BMP Production for ABRSM

Contents

Introduction

In the exam

Overview of Grade 4 & 5 aural tests

Grade 4 aural tests

Test 4A Melodic repetition

Test 4B Sight-singing

Test 4C (i) Musical features

(ii) Rhythmic repetition and metre

Grade 5 aural tests

Introduction

Developing listening skills

Musical learning, as with language learning, begins with the ear and not with the eye. For children to be able to speak and understand language, they need to listen carefully to the talking that is going on around them. The skills of reading and writing, which are dependent on the eye, come later in the learning process. For musicians, similarly, listening is the first and foremost activity, and – whether it is listening to their own playing or to that of others – it lies at the heart of all good music-making. Listening skills are therefore fundamental to any musical training programme, especially one which aims to develop performance skills.

First, though, it would be useful to define what is meant by listening, and how it differs from hearing. While hearing happens automatically whenever the ear receives sound, listening is a conscious act which requires active concentration. To illustrate this difference to your students you might ask them to close their eyes and listen to how many sounds they can notice and identify. Many of the sounds around them will only become apparent when they listen; the ears had been hearing them, but the brain had not perceived them. This could be thought of as the aural equivalent of the situation in which Sherlock Holmes says to his assistant, Dr Watson, 'You see, but you do not observe.'

The three volumes of *Aural Training in Practice* are all about helping your students to develop listening skills, or what is sometimes called a 'musical ear'. Many resources refer to this process as 'ear training' – even though it is actually the brain and not the ear itself that is being trained! Other terms that you may also come across are 'inner ear', 'aural imagination' and 'audiation'. While these might seem rather abstract, the basic activity to which they all refer – hearing sounds in your head – is of crucial importance to musicians. It allows them to hear and perceive music for which the physical sound is not necessarily present at all. The process of hearing music in your head may happen when listening to it, imagining it, score-reading, singing, playing from notation, playing by ear, improvising, composing or writing music down.

Having a good musical ear and well-developed listening skills enhances all aspects of musicianship, including:

- **awareness of your own playing**
  feeling for musical shape and direction, sense of phrase lengths and balance, tonal balance between registers (or between hands on the piano)

- **playing or singing in tune**
  sense of what is sharp and what is flat intonation, ability to tune your instrument to another, awareness of the need to adjust pitch according to context

- **balancing and blending with other musicians**
  ensemble awareness, keeping together, understanding your role within the overall texture, attending to other parts as well as your own

- **playing rhythmically and expressively**
  feeling for pulse and metre, sensitivity to tempo and tempo changes, ability to be flexible with pulse, dynamic awareness, tonal sensitivity

- **memorizing music**
  hearing the music in your head, learning cues from other parts, recognizing harmonic structure and patterns

- **fluency and accuracy in sight-reading**
  interpreting notation and knowing in advance how the music should sound, in order to keep going

Of course, there are many different ways in which the musical ear can be developed, especially via practical musical activities which rely particularly on listening. These are very much at the heart of the *Aural Training in Practice* volumes. Whether the activities help with clapping the beat or echo singing skills at Grade 1, or with identifying chords and modulations correctly at Grade 8, the basic underlying aim is always the same: to develop all-round musicianship skills through aural training.

Aural skills and singing

Singing is particularly effective in training the musical ear. Often when you imagine what music sounds like, you are effectively singing it in your head, whether or not you vocalize the sound. But singing out loud actually strengthens the aural imagination and makes a direct and vital connection between the internal imagining of sound and its external realization.

With singing there is no need to find a note on an instrument; important though that physical connection can be, it can get in the way of expressing musical ideas that have already formed internally. Singing can improve many aspects of your students' musicianship, including their sense of pitch, intonation, phrasing and articulation, so it is well worth encouraging, even when you have a reluctant singer. Getting students to sing back musical material that has been internalized is also an important way in which listening skills can be evaluated, because it provides a direct way for you, as their teacher, to gauge your students' aural perception and awareness.

Integrating aural training into the lesson

If practical aural activities are threaded in imaginative ways through every lesson, preparation for the aural tests within an exam becomes a natural extension of what is already a central part of students' musical learning. If, on the other hand, aural tests are regarded more as a series of 'hoops to be jumped through', preparation for which might be left until only a few weeks before an exam, or given just a few minutes per lesson, there is a real risk that students' aural potential will remain unrealized.

One of the most effective ways to make aural training a fun and interesting part of your lessons is to use the music that your student is working on as a basis for developing aural skills. Its melodies and phrases, its harmony and tonality, its rhythm and metre, and its musical and expressive detail can all become starting points for aural activities which make the connection between learning a piece and developing aural skills.

For the purposes of assessment in ABRSM Practical graded music exams, different elements such as aural, sight-reading, performance and technical work are treated separately. In the context of teaching and learning, however, these need to be much more interconnected. Developing aural skills is a central feature of all effective instrumental or vocal lessons, and should not be set apart from other aspects of learning. Every moment of active, focused listening in lessons, as well as during practice sessions, is valuable in helping to develop aural skills.

Direct connections can also be made between the development of aural skills and the theoretical side of musical understanding. When a new concept of music theory is introduced, understanding can be supported by the aural realization of what it sounds like in practice. This is equally the case whether you are introducing a new time signature at a low grade or exploring modulations at the higher grades. Studying music theory, grade-by-grade, is useful here, and a wide range of resources is available to help the teaching and learning of music theory to progress in a structured and systematic manner. Likewise, at each step of the way, knowledge and understanding of musical elements (e.g. time signatures, major and minor keys, cadences or modulations) will support and enhance the acquisition of related aural skills (i.e. recognizing the metre, hearing the difference between tonalities, identifying the 'sound signature' of a cadence or hearing the 'tonal journey' of a modulation).

There are many different ways in which aural skills can be integrated with all areas of music teaching and learning. The teaching hints and strategies in this book provide useful starting points, but they are by no means comprehensive. The context of the individual student, and the music he or she is working on, should determine the strategies you use.

Why examine aural skills?

ABRSM Practical graded music exams are more than just instrumental or vocal exams – they are *music* exams, and they support the development of all-round musicianship. They provide an assessment and a record of achievement not only in performing a range of repertoire but also in demonstrating wider musical skills against the standard set for the grade. The exams give students a clear indication of their progress, and they are therefore often regarded as milestones which mark the journey of the developing musician.

Although aural skills are of course involved throughout the exam, the focal point when it comes to assessing the candidate's musical ear is the aural tests. The underlying purpose and value of the tests, and thereby also of the activities preparing a student for them, is to inform and enhance the student's all-round development as a musician. While the tests themselves take only a few minutes, they tell the examiner a great deal about the candidate's broader musicianship.

Aural training for non-pianists

Although only some candidates will be taking piano exams, aural tests for all instrumentalists and singers are delivered using the piano. Not only does this permit a full range of harmony, texture and tessitura for music examples, but it means that the tests are played live, like the rest of the exam. This gives the opportunity for musical interaction between examiner and candidate and keeps the emphasis on listening to live performance, which lies at the heart of all ABRSM Practical exams.

Although the piano will be used in the exam (and students should therefore be comfortable and familiar with responding to tests played on the piano), all the Grade 1–5 tests can be prepared to some extent using any melody instrument, or the voice, and do not necessarily rely on the use of a piano. Teachers are strongly encouraged to develop aural skills in their lessons through the instrument being learnt. It would be misleading to give students the impression that the development of aural skills is only piano-based, and it is important to realize that up to Grade 5 all the aural tests can be usefully practised by using any melody instrument.

The scope of this book

This book is designed primarily as a resource for you to use when preparing your students for ABRSM aural tests. While sound educational principles inform the range and choice of aural skills tested, aural tests in an exam inevitably have certain limitations in scope. You should therefore regard the advice and exercises presented in this book as serving the specific needs of exam preparation. They are not a substitute for a broad curriculum of general aural training, for which many different approaches and programmes can be found, together with supporting publications and online resources. You will no doubt be already aware of additional materials of this kind that are appropriate to your style of working and to your students' individual needs.

What is in the book?

Overview of Grade 4 and 5 aural tests

This sets out the educational and musical purpose and value of each activity. Where appropriate, it also explains the relationship to tests found at the earlier grades. It gives a sense of the progression from Grade 4 to Grade 5, and shows how the skills that are assessed relate to fundamental aspects of musical learning.

Grade 4 and 5 aural tests

At a glance
For ease of reference, a table is provided at the start of every grade giving a brief summary of each of the tests.

What the test involves
This section begins with a description of the test, as given in the syllabus. Also provided here is the rubric – the form of words used by examiners when delivering the aural tests. If your students are familiar with these rubrics before their exam, there is much less chance of misunderstanding or confusion on the day. This section also covers any practical aspects of how the test is run and, where appropriate, explains what the examiner is looking for.

The basic parameters, such as the pitch range or maximum number of bars, are given for each test so that you can devise or select your own material to create tests of a similar level to those in the exam.

Teaching hints and strategies
These are intended to be useful for stimulating ideas and suggesting possible preparation activities and teaching approaches. They show how the various tests can be broken down into their component parts, and how they can be linked to examples from music the student is currently studying – both as a developing performer and as a listener. As stated earlier, if you use the music your students are learning as the basis for aural work, it will help to focus their listening and make aural development as enjoyable, relevant, worthwhile and effective as possible.

Please note that for the purposes of this book some of the music extracts used in these sections and in the practice exercises have been freely adapted.

Practice exercises
These illustrate the kind of material that will be used in the exam. For some tests, the first of the practice exercises given may be a little easier than those later on in the section, so that students can gain confidence with the activity from the outset. Also, the tests at the end of

the section might be a little harder or longer than those that could come up in the exam itself, enabling you to stretch and challenge even the strongest of your students.

The examiner rubric is printed at the start of each set of tests and at the top of any subsequent left-hand pages, so that you can present the tests to your students in a way that helps prepare them for the exam experience. Volumes of *Specimen Aural Tests* offer further practice material which can provide the basis for running mock exams.

The practice exercises are designed to be generally manageable by teachers for whom the piano may not be their first study, but who are able to play at around Grade 5 level. However, to help teachers who are non-pianists and to provide opportunities for students to practise the tests away from lessons, all the exercises are included on the accompanying CD.

A copy of the practice exercises for the sight-singing tests (Tests 4B and 5B) is provided on a separate sheet for the student to use.

Answers

Model answers for the practice exercises for Tests 4C(i) and 5C(i) are given on pp. 54–55, as a guide to the sort of responses that would be successful in the exam. Answers are also given on the CD for any parts of the tests that require a spoken response. In some cases there are other ways of responding that would be equally successful, so the answers should be used only as a guide. It should also be noted that in an exam the examiner will not provide answers.

CD

The accompanying CD includes recordings of any music examples in two or more parts that appear within the teaching hints sections, which will be particularly useful for those teachers who do not have access to a keyboard or who are non-pianists. It also includes all the practice exercises in this book, along with the spoken rubrics. The practice exercises on the CD are delivered by an ABRSM examiner, in order to match the exam experience as closely as possible. The CD may also help in enabling students to practise aural tests between lessons. Answers are given for all tests that require a spoken response. For tests that require a sung response, there is an opportunity to check the response. Silent gaps are provided where appropriate to give students the opportunity to answer, but if extra thinking time is required the recording may simply be paused.

Track numbers are printed at the start of each recorded music example, and a track list is provided on p. 56.

Further recorded examples can be found within the volumes of *Specimen Aural Tests* with CD, which also include a sample mock aural test for each grade. These mock tests are also available as free downloads from www.abrsm.org/mockauraltests.

In the exam

Practicalities

The aural tests are conducted by the examiner at the piano. They can be taken at any stage of the exam at the candidate's request, although most candidates take this section last. However, even though candidates can choose when they take the aural tests, they cannot change the order of the tests themselves.

Candidates should face the examiner, in a position where the piano keyboard cannot be seen. If necessary, examiners will tell candidates where to stand, and put them at their ease before starting the aural tests. Candidates with portable instruments will often need to put down their instrument before the tests begin.

Each test will be delivered following a fixed set of spoken words or instructions (the examiner rubric). All music extracts will be played on the piano, and the examiner will be ready to prompt if necessary where there is hesitation or where clarification is needed.

For Test B, candidates will be given their own copy of the music to be sung, which will be retrieved by the examiner before the next test.

Giving answers

Clapping

Clapped responses need to be clear and well projected. It might be worth asking your students to experiment with tapping two or three fingers of one hand against the palm of the other. This maximizes the clarity of sound, allows the strong beats or stresses to be communicated easily, and can permit more agility when repeating shorter note-values.

Playing

Melodic repetition tests (Tests 4A and 5A) offer candidates the opportunity to respond on the piano or their own instrument, as an alternative to singing. Candidates may play their response at a different octave if appropriate.

If the melody is to be repeated on a transposing instrument, the key-chord and starting note named by the examiner will be appropriate to the instrument in question, enabling the test to be played back at the correct sounding pitch. For example, if the melody is in F major and starts on A, a candidate playing a horn in F will be told that the key-chord is C major and the starting note is E whereas, for the same piece, a candidate playing a clarinet in B♭ would be told that the key-chord is G major and the starting note is B.

Singing/humming/whistling

For any test that requires a sung response it is pitch rather than vocal quality that is being assessed. Responses may be sung to any vowel (or consonant followed by a vowel), or hummed or whistled (and at a different octave, if appropriate). Students who are less comfortable singing often find that humming is their best option in the exam. Whatever method is used, it is helpful to respond confidently and loudly enough to be heard clearly. If candidates respond tentatively, they do not give themselves the best chance to hear their own pitching clearly, and the sound may then also lack conviction.

In sight-singing tests candidates may wish to use sol-fa note names or letter names of the notes when they sing, if this is helpful to them. It is perfectly acceptable in the exam for candidates to vocalize the notes in any way they wish. For these tests, candidates may choose to sing from treble or bass clef.

Usually the music for melodic repetition tests will be played in a medium treble register, but students should feel free to request it to be played in a different register if this would be more comfortable. Examiners will be happy to match tests to the vocal range of the candidate, and are sympathetic to changing and adolescent voices that can have a narrow or unpredictable range. Any helpful information supplied by the candidate such as 'I would like this played in a bass register' or 'I currently have a voice range of F up to middle C' is welcome. It is useful to make sure that any student with specific pitch requirements knows how to tell the examiner about them, and knows to do so before the aural tests begin.

Speaking

Where tests involve a spoken response, candidates should be encouraged to speak clearly and confidently, though the examiner will be sympathetic to different approaches to verbal communication – the emphasis being on assessing musical perception as expressed in the candidate's own words. Candidates are encouraged to use Italian terms where appropriate but there will be no disadvantage to those who do not, provided that their response is equally clear and accurate.

Any candidate who is not comfortable using English is permitted to bring an interpreter into the exam room in accordance with ABRSM regulations.

Second attempts

In some tests, such as Tests A and B at Grades 4 and 5, examiners have discretion to allow a second attempt if necessary. However, the need for a second attempt will be taken into account in the assessment.

How are the aural tests marked?

The mark for aural tests is arrived at by making an overall assessment of the candidate's performance during the set of tests as a whole, and relating this to the assessment criteria shown below. Rather than starting at zero and awarding marks as the tests proceed, or at 18 and then deducting marks, examiners apply a principle of marking positively or negatively from the pass mark. The mark then reflects the cumulative balance of strengths and weaknesses that the candidate has demonstrated, taking into account the accuracy, perceptiveness and quality of the responses given.

Assessment criteria (all grades)

	Distinction
(18)	• Quick, accurate and perceptive responses

	Merit
(15–17)	• Good responses
	• Minor errors or hesitation

	Pass
(12–14)	• Approximately half the tests correctly answered
	• Evidence of awareness, despite hesitation and error

Below Pass

(9–11)
- Slow and uncertain responses
- Inaccuracy in parts of all tests

(6–8)
- Very slow and mostly incorrect responses
- All tests entirely inaccurate

(0)
- No work offered

Access (for candidates with specific needs)

Deaf or hearing-impaired candidates may opt to respond to alternative tests in place of the standard tests, if requested at the time of entry. The syllabus for these tests is available free on request from ABRSM. For blind or partially-sighted candidates, alternative tests are available for Test B. For further information about alternative tests and access for candidates with specific needs please contact ABRSM's Access Co-ordinator or visit the website.

Telephone +44 (0)20 7636 5400
Textphone +44 (0)20 7637 2582
Email accesscoordinator@abrsm.ac.uk
www.abrsm.org/specialneeds

Overview of Grade 4 and 5 aural tests

The aural activities at Grades 4 and 5 continue to focus on areas that will be familiar from the earlier grades: rhythm, pitch and awareness of basic musical features such as dynamics, articulation, tempo and major/minor key. But there is now a greater emphasis on the ability to think in sound, and the demands of aural perception and musical awareness are also increased, with candidates being expected to make more sophisticated observations about musical features. Building on the foundations established at Grades 1–3, the aim of the aural tests at Grades 4 and 5 is to encourage further development of the candidate's musical ear.

The tests at Grades 4 and 5 can be summarized as:

Test A   Melodic repetition

Test B   Sight-singing

Test C   (i) Musical features
(ii) Rhythmic repetition and metre

Test A   Melodic repetition

This test builds on the echo singing tests in Grades 1–3. The candidate is required to sing or play a short melody from memory, after hearing it twice. The melodies for the Grade 5 tests are generally longer and slightly more complex than those at Grade 4, but otherwise similar. Candidates have the option of singing (or humming or whistling) back the melody, or of playing it back on the piano or their own instrument. The test aims to develop not only melodic memory but also the ability to think in sound, one of the foundations of musicianship.

In some ways, melodic repetition integrates the mind with the body, helping your students to develop the skill of hearing a melody in their head and then turning that internal musical 'image' back into physical sound via their instrument or voice. Being able to internalize a melody and then to reproduce it accurately is a very valuable skill. It helps musicians to perceive a phrase as a complete musical 'sentence', rather than just a series of notes or 'words' – something which is crucial for expressive musical communication.

Test B   Sight-singing

This test requires the candidate to sing (or hum or whistle) at sight from notation. The process of imagining the pitch of notes which are yet to be sounded is an important aspect of thinking in sound, and helps musicians to detect and correct errors when learning new music. Sight-singing is a highly effective way of developing this skill because the link between symbol and sound is not hampered by the need to make a physical movement by playing notes on an instrument. Of course, some physical movements are needed to sing, but these are more natural and instinctive than those required to play an instrument.

At Grades 4 and 5 the test involves pitch only, since this is a logical starting point, and the possible range and intervals are limited at each grade, so as to build skills progressively.

Test C (i) Musical features; (ii) Rhythmic repetition and metre

The first part of this test is an extension of Test D at Grades 1–3, in which the candidate is required to listen to a short piece of music played on the piano and to answer questions about it. At Grades 4 and 5, there is an emphasis on assessing the candidate's understanding of how music achieves its effects. So, in addition to considering features such as dynamics, articulation, tempo and major/minor key, which were covered at the earlier grades, candidates at Grade 4 are asked about the character of the music, and at Grade 5 about its style and period. The focus of questions is not only on being able to describe the character of the piece or to name the style or period, but also on being able to identify the features of the music which point to those conclusions.

Appreciating and responding to music and its expressive qualities is a very personal experience, and one which is often not easy to put into words. But students who listen attentively to music and who learn to recognize which features give it its character, or indicate its style and period, become more able to communicate those features in their own playing or singing. Expressive communication, as opposed to the mere observance of printed notation, is what brings a piece of music to life in performance, and awareness of stylistic features and historical context becomes increasingly important as students progress and begin to make their own informed interpretative decisions.

The second part of this test is an extension of the 'pulse and metre' test (Test A in the earlier grades). It requires the candidate to clap back the rhythm of the notes from a phrase taken from the piece already heard, and to identify the metre. This encourages students to develop further their aural memory and – importantly, for success in performance – their sense of inner pulse, rhythm and metre. The rhythm to be clapped at Grade 5 will be slightly longer and/or more complex than the rhythm at Grade 4.

Grade 4 aural tests

At a glance

Test 4A	**Melodic repetition**

Sing or play from memory a melody heard twice.

Test 4B	**Sight-singing**

Sing five notes from score in free time.

Test 4C	**(i) Musical features**

Listen to a piece and answer questions about dynamics, articulation, tempo change or tonality, and about character.

(ii) Rhythmic repetition and metre

Clap the rhythm of a short extract heard twice, and then identify the metre.

Test 4A   Melodic repetition

What the test involves

Syllabus description:

> **To sing or play from memory a melody played twice by the examiner.** The melody will be within the range of an octave, in a major or minor key with up to three sharps or flats. First the examiner will play the key-chord and the starting note and then count in two bars. (If the candidate chooses to play, the examiner will also name the key-chord and the starting note, as appropriate for the instrument.) If necessary, the examiner will play the melody again and allow a second attempt (although this will affect the assessment).

Examiner rubric:

> *Here is a melody for you to repeat. Would you prefer to sing it or play it? ... I'll play it twice. Here is the key-chord* [play] *and your starting note* [play]*.* [Count in two bars, then play the melody once.] *Here it is again.* [Repeat the melody without counting in.] *... Thank you.*

The melody will begin on a note from the tonic triad and will not include any chromatic notes. It will be no more than four bars long in two time (including 6/8), three time or four time.

Many of the melodies include articulation, and all have a dynamic marking. Candidates may reflect the articulation and dynamic in their response if they wish. For the purposes of the exam, however, accuracy of pitch and rhythm are the only elements which the examiner will assess in this test.

For further guidance on responding to this test, see Playing and Singing/humming/whistling on pp. 10–11.

Teaching hints and strategies

Students who have taken the earlier grades will already be familiar with many of the preparation activities that will be useful for this test, such as those provided for the echo tests at Grades 1 to 3. A helpful preliminary exercise is to separate the rhythm from the pitch by giving your students a rhythm to clap back. You can start with something relatively straightforward and then gradually increase the difficulty:

Once your students become comfortable repeating more demanding rhythms, move on to pitch. Most musicians find it easier to sing a tune that they have just heard than to play it, so it is not surprising that candidates usually choose to sing rather than play their response to this test. For the majority of students this is a more immediate and secure way of responding. However, it is good to encourage all your students to practise both singing and playing back the melody, as this will strengthen their aural awareness and broaden their musicianship skills. Hints on how to develop the necessary skills for each type of response are given below.

If you are beginning with sung responses, you might choose one of the rhythms above, or something similar, and ask your student to repeat it on a single pitch of his or her choice. After this you could ask your student to sing back a rhythm, still on a monotone, but perhaps at a pitch that you select.

Before trying to sing back a melody, it may be useful for your student to sing up and down the scale and arpeggio in the key of the melody to help establish the tonal context. Most melodies use neighbouring notes at some point, and being able to recognize stepwise motion helps with memorization. Rather than always singing the scale and arpeggio separately, your student could combine aspects of both by singing up and down the scale (perhaps major first then minor) but holding on to the notes of the tonic triad a little longer, as shown in this example:

This has the benefit of encouraging aural awareness of how the scale and the arpeggio are related and helps to develop a sense of the characteristic quality and relative significance of each degree of the scale. The exercise is useful, therefore, even if your student is intending to play rather than sing back the melody.

For students who choose to sing back the melody, the initial challenge is often remembering the right starting pitch. All examples will start (and often end) on a note from the tonic triad, so exercises that reinforce awareness of the three notes of the tonic triad, such as the one suggested above, will help here.

Some students may find it easier at first to respond to sung rather than played examples, because of the closer match between the sounds. You might also try playing the phrases to your students on the instrument they are learning, to integrate preparation for this test more naturally and effectively into lessons. However, students will eventually need to become at ease with responding to the piano, as this is how the test will be delivered in the exam.

A good way to develop the skills needed to play back the melody is to encourage your students to play well-known traditional and popular tunes by ear. Begin with simple melodies to gain confidence. Using television theme tunes that have been heard many times can make this a fun activity, but other sources such as folk or pop songs, hymn tunes or nursery rhymes can also provide useful material. Alternatively, you could play part of a phrase from a piece that your student is learning, and see if he or she can play it back without the notation. Encourage students to visualize which fingerings they would use on their instrument as they listen to the melody. This will help them make that vital physical connection between the sound and the action needed to reproduce it.

For all of the preparatory examples given here, and for any that you create of your own, it is a good idea to introduce the example by giving the key-chord and starting note, then counting in two bars. This will help your students place the phrase within its tonal context, and grasp how the rhythm fits with the pulse.

Singing or playing back melodies that begin and end on the tonic using simple, regular rhythms and small intervals is a good starting point for gradually building up to the sort of phrase found in the exam.

Next, you might try some examples that begin and end on the 3rd or 5th note of the scale, as this gently increases the challenge. Notice that these examples also include some larger intervals as well as leaps of a 3rd between notes that are not part of the tonic triad.

Now move on to examples with more complex rhythms. First, ask your students to listen to a phrase and clap back the rhythm. Once they have reproduced the rhythm correctly, play the phrase twice more and this time ask them to sing or play the pitches to the rhythm.

As your students' confidence and skill increase, you can gradually introduce a wider range of rhythms and extend the pitch range to an octave. Although phrases will always begin on one of the key-chord notes, the final note does not have to be from the tonic triad, so include some examples that end on other notes of the scale. You could alter the last few notes of examples already given as a gentle way in before trying the melodies below. Where the melody begins with an upbeat, such as in the second and third examples, make the natural rhythmic emphasis clear both in your count-in and in your playing, stressing the first strong beat to help your student make full sense of the melodic shape.

Your students should now be ready to try the practice exercises. Encourage them to sing or play back the melody immediately – almost like one of the echoes in the earlier grades. With any delay in response, memory tends to fade and sense of pulse can be lost, often leading to a less certain or reliable outcome than one which is prompt.

Practice exercises

Here is a melody for you to repeat. Would you prefer to sing it or play it?* *... I'll play it twice. Here is the key-chord* [play] *and your starting note* [play]**.** [Count in two bars, then play the melody once.] *Here it is again.* [Repeat the melody without counting in.] *... Thank you.*

* [If the candidate chooses to play, name as well as play the key-chord and starting note. With transposing instruments use only the examples specified, naming the key-chord and starting note as shown, according to the instrument.]

1   **Andante**   Schumann

Transposing instruments **in B♭**: E minor, starting note E; **in F**: A minor, starting note A; **in E♭**: B minor, starting note B

2   **Allegretto**   Mendelssohn

3   **Andante**   English folksong

Transposing instruments **in B♭**: E minor, starting note E; **in F**: A minor, starting note A; **in E♭**: B minor, starting note B

4   **Moderato**   Weber

Transposing instruments **in B♭**: G major, starting note D; **in F**: C major, starting note G; **in E♭**: D major, starting note A

5   **Moderato**   Bizet

Transposing instruments **in B♭**: D minor, starting note D; **in F**: G minor, starting note G; **in E♭**: A minor, starting note A

6   **Moderato**   Folksong

Transposing instruments **in B♭**: G major, starting note G; **in F**: C major, starting note C; **in E♭**: D major, starting note D

7   **Andante**   Mozart

Transposing instruments **in B♭**: F major, starting note C; **in F**: B♭ major, starting note F; **in E♭**: C major, starting note G

8   **Andante**   Schubert

Transposing instruments **in B♭**: A major, starting note A; **in F**: D major, starting note D

Test 4B Sight-singing

What the test involves

Syllabus description:

To sing five notes from score in free time. The candidate may choose to sing from treble or bass clef. The notes will be within the range of a 3rd above and below the tonic in the key of C, F or G major. The test will begin and end on the tonic and will not contain intervals greater than a 3rd. First the examiner will name and play the key-chord and the starting note. If necessary, the examiner will help the candidate by playing and identifying the correct note if any note is sung at the wrong pitch.

Examiner rubric:

[When appropriate: *Would you prefer to sing notes in treble clef or bass clef?*] *Please sing the notes at number ... on this page. Sing them slowly, and I'll help by giving you the right note if you sing a wrong one. Here is the key-chord* [name and play] *and this is your starting note* [name and play]. *... Thank you.*

A pulse is not given for this test, enabling candidates to choose their speed as well as allowing 'thinking time' between notes, if needed.

For further guidance on responding to this test, see Singing/humming/whistling on pp. 10–11.

Teaching hints and strategies

As this test is limited in terms of pitch range and will not include intervals greater than a 3rd, the potential challenges can be easily broken down as follows:

1) moving up and down from the tonic by step

2) leaping by a 3rd within the range of five notes

You could begin by working on the first of these, singing three notes up and down from the tonic by step and asking your student to echo the pattern back while following the notes on the page. Some teachers will want to incorporate sol-fa names when preparing this with their students, while others might encourage their students to sing the letter names. There are several different ways to approach this, and it is perfectly acceptable in the exam for candidates to vocalize the notes in any way they wish; there is no requirement to sing note names.

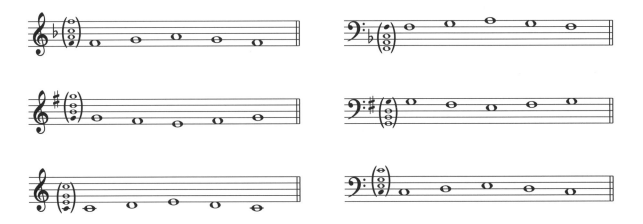

Once your student is confident with this exercise and can sing these patterns in the three keys without any help, you can move on to working on the second challenge – intervals of a 3rd, both major and minor. In this test the major 3rd is between the tonic and mediant notes, and the minor 3rd is between the tonic and submediant notes or between the leading note and supertonic. In F major, for example, the possibilities are as follows:

The minor 3rd is a natural 'calling' interval – often familiar through playground games or nursery rhymes, as well as via the cuckoo call. It is also the first interval introduced by the Kodály method. The major 3rd is perhaps best internalized as the first two notes of a major triad or arpeggio (in root position) or, in the context of this test, the lower two notes of the key-chord which the candidate will hear just before beginning the test.

A simple echo exercise is a good way to help your student learn the sound and 'feel' of these two intervals. You could start with just one type, then move on to mixing them up. Sing the interval(s) and ask your student to echo back while following the notes.

Major 3rds

Minor 3rds

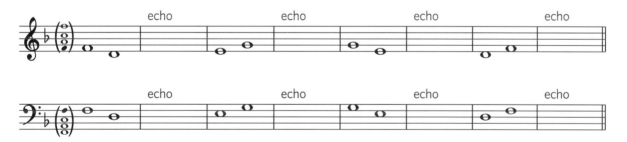

Major and minor 3rds

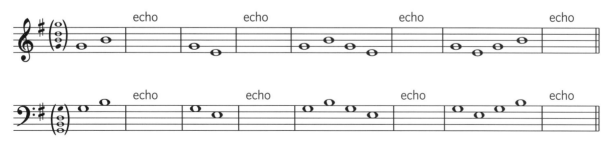

Devising other similar practice exercises involving 3rds should be quite straightforward.

Next you might combine movement-by-step with movement-by-leap, as shown in the exercises below. As before, students should practise these by giving echo responses while following the notes.

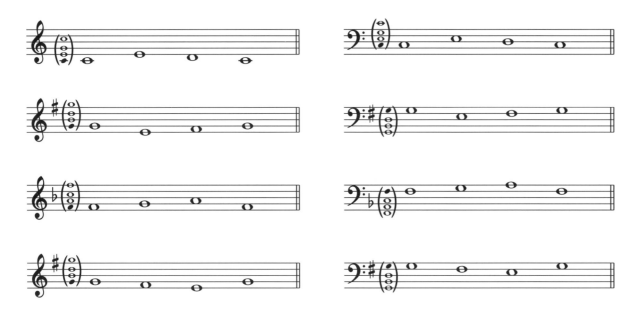

Only one more note needs adding to bring these preliminary exercises up to full length, perhaps combining one or both types of 3rd with some stepwise movement:

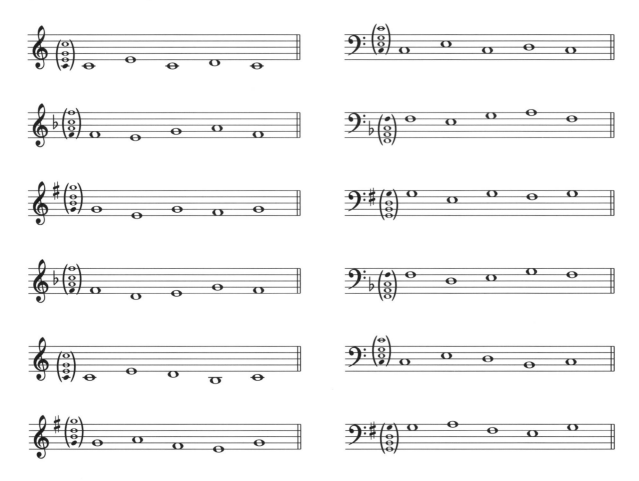

The next step should be for your student to hear the intervals in his or her head, then to sing them at sight. In the early stages it might be helpful to 'shadow' the singing by playing each note once it has been attempted, to make sure that the next note is gauged from one which is correct and in tune. This also mirrors the way in which examiners will help by giving the correct note if they feel it is needed to get the best response from a candidate. However, many candidates will have no difficulty here and, once the key-chord and starting note have been given, will sing the notes without needing help.

Encourage your students to sing confidently, as a note sung quietly or tentatively will not provide a firm launch-pad from which to aim for the next note. Holding each note for a reasonable length of time – perhaps a couple of seconds – will help to ensure certainty of pitch. (In the exam, this will also enable the examiner to help by playing the right note if the pitching is incorrect.)

Practice exercises

[When appropriate: *Would you prefer to sing notes in treble or bass clef?*] *Please sing the notes at number ... on this page. Sing them slowly, and I'll help by giving you the right note if you sing a wrong one. Here is the key-chord* [name and play] *and this is your starting note* [name and play]*. ... Thank you.*

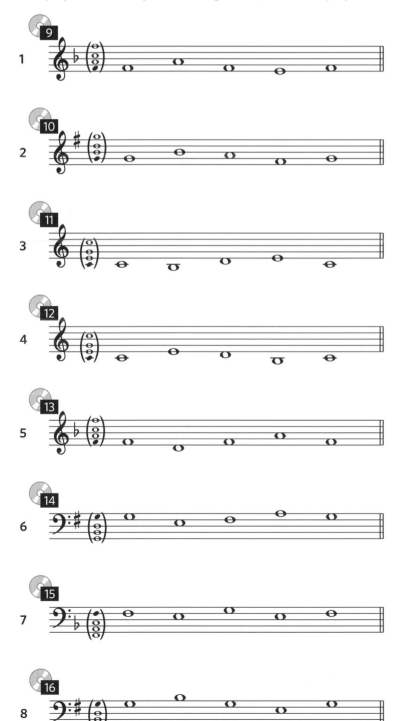

Test 4C (i) Musical features

What the test involves

Syllabus description:

> **To answer questions about two features of a piece played by the examiner.** Before playing, the examiner will tell the candidate which two features the questions will be about. The first will be *one* of the following: dynamics, articulation, tempo, tonality; the second will be character.

Examiner rubric:

> *Listen to this piece, then I'll ask you about …* [choose one of the first three features listed below the piece] *and about character.* [After playing, ask one question at a time.]

This test builds on questions asked at earlier grades in Test D about dynamics, articulation, tempo and tonality. Note that from Grade 4 onwards examiners will sometimes refer to these features by name, without using explanatory terms such as 'loud and quiet playing' or 'smooth and detached notes'.

In addition to answering a question on one of these features, candidates will be asked to say what gives the music its particular character. They therefore need to do more than describe the character of the music; they must also identify musical features that contribute to the character in question. This demonstrates more objective perception and understanding, beyond an essentially subjective opinion. In answering this question candidates usually begin by describing the features that have been most noticeable to them, which then leads them to a conclusion about the music's overall character.

The examiner is looking for a ready, confident response that shows perceptive awareness of the relevant musical features.

For further guidance on responding to this part of the test, see Speaking on p. 11.

Teaching hints and strategies

Tests in the early grades require students to distinguish between loud and quiet dynamic levels, smooth and detached articulation, and major and minor key, and to detect changes of tempo within a piece of music. At Grades 4 and 5 questions on these areas are slightly more challenging. For example, candidates might now be asked to describe the dynamics, rather than being asked more specific questions such as whether the first half was louder than the second. Similarly, questions about articulation might now focus on a specific part of the texture, such as accompanying chords or the melodic line. Teaching hints and strategies for all these areas are contained in *Aural Training in Practice*, Grades 1–3, which provides a useful resource for any students needing some revision.

The new element at Grade 4 is that candidates will be asked to account for the character of the music (such as happy or sad, lively or calm). To a certain extent the character of music is a subjective matter, as everyone responds to music individually. However, the piece in the exam will have a distinct musical character which many candidates will recognize easily. It is well worth helping your students to develop a ready vocabulary of useful words to describe musical character. As the grades progress, the range and sophistication of this vocabulary will need to increase. Eventually, by Grade 8, students are expected to describe the music without prompting from the examiner, so this test at Grade 4 is an important starting point.

The following extract from 'The Sick Doll' (from *Album for the Young*, Op. 39) by Tchaikovsky would be described by most candidates as sad or serious, although other descriptive words such as calm would also be appropriate. The moderate tempo, minor key and falling melodic phrases all contribute to its sombre mood, and it is features such as these that candidates need to identify.

In contrast, the extract from the Major-General's Song (from *The Pirates of Penzance* by Gilbert and Sullivan) has a happy, lively mood, owing to its brisk tempo, major key and fast-running quavers.

Describing the overall character of a piece may not present much difficulty to your students, but identifying the specific musical features which contribute to that character may well need practice.

The character of the following piece, a cheeky version of the jolly nursery rhyme 'Bobby Shafto's gone to sea', is bright and cheerful. You might ask your students what makes it sound bright and cheerful, and then discuss some of the relevant features, such as the lively tempo, the jazzy rhythms, the use of staccato and the loud ending.

Extract from 'Bonny Bobby Bluetoe', No. 10 from *Swinging Rhymes*
© 1991 by The Associated Board of the Royal Schools of Music

Now try this one. Its gentle mood is created by a slowish tempo, lilting rhythms and smooth phrasing.

It is worth noting here that minor key does not always mean sad mood, and that it is the combined effect of musical features which gives a piece its character. The following piece, although in a minor key, certainly doesn't sound sad. The combination of rapid rising notes, high register and use of staccato gives the music a lively, sprightly character.

Asking your students to give you some adjectives that describe the musical ideas contained in pieces they are learning will help them to think about the elements of music and how they combine to give music character. Take, for example, the first two ideas of this Scherzo by J. C. F. Bach:

You could ask your student: 'How many words can you find to describe the first musical idea?'. He or she might answer with some of the following: major key, staccato, contrary motion, playful, loud, arpeggiated. The second idea is almost the exact opposite of this and the adjectives might be: minor key, smooth, similar motion, serious, quiet, stepwise.

Thinking about how the individual characteristics of musical ideas can be described is a useful way to connect musical features with the emotional aspects of music. The ability to characterize musical ideas is an increasingly significant skill in successful performance from Grade 4 onwards, so encouraging your students to think about musical character in their pieces presents an ideal opportunity for you to integrate aural training with related work being done in the lesson.

Test 4C   (ii) Rhythmic repetition and metre

What the test involves

Syllabus description:

> **To clap the rhythm of the notes in an extract from the same piece** [as for part (i)], **and to identify whether it is in two time, three time or four time.** The examiner will play the extract twice (unharmonized), after which the candidate should clap back the rhythm. The examiner will then ask whether the music is in two time, three time or four time. The candidate is *not* required to state the time signature.

Examiner rubric:

> ***Now clap the rhythm of the notes in this phrase, after I've played it twice more.*** [Play the extract once.] ***Here it is again.*** [Repeat the extract.] *... **Is it in two time, three time or four time?** ... **Thank you.***

The rhythm to be clapped will be up to approximately four bars in two or three time, or two bars in four time. Although a piece may be in 6/8 (the only compound time signature used in Test 4C), the candidate should identify it as being in two time.

For further guidance on responding to this part of the test, see Clapping on p. 10.

Teaching hints and strategies

To prepare for this part of the test, it is a good idea to start with some relatively simple exercises. You might begin by asking your student to echo a rhythm that you clap:

Next, try a slightly more complex rhythm:

Then dotted rhythms and notes of shorter value can be introduced:

Now try something similar, but play the rhythm on a single note on the piano or another instrument:

The next stage is to play a single melodic line, without accompaniment, and ask your student to clap its rhythm. Alternatively, you can make it more like the exam experience by first playing the melody with its accompaniment. Take the opening section of this Menuet by Leopold Mozart, for example:

Having played the music through, and perhaps explored some of its features, you could ask your student to clap the rhythm of the first half of the melody, after playing it twice:

If this proves too challenging, simply go back a stage and work on shorter or simpler phrases. For example, the phrase above could be split into two halves, each starting with an upbeat.

In the early stages it can be useful to give a count-in. Although this obviously gives away the metre of the music – which students will eventually have to recognize by themselves – it also provides the underlying pulse of the rhythm to be memorized and clapped. This can be particularly important when the rhythm includes longer note values, such as in this example by Fauré:

By keeping the pulse in mind, students can avoid the common tendency to rush the clapping by inadvertently cutting long notes short.

As a preliminary exercise in identifying metre, you could play some music and ask your students to clap the beat, giving greater emphasis to the first beat of the bar, in the manner of Test A at Grades 1–3. The next stage would be for your students to imagine the pulse – perhaps also gently tapping a foot or wiggling a toe to start with (something they could do in the exam). This process of internalizing the pulse is necessary in order to perceive the metre. Make sure that you include some examples in 6/8, to check that your students recognize the typical triplet rhythms and feel the metre as two in a bar.

Although the examiner asks for the metre at the end of the test, you should encourage your students to try to gain an idea of the metre when the whole piece is played during the first part of the test, since it is usually more obvious when heard in context. Having an idea of the metre ahead of the rhythmic repetition test also helps to make musical sense of the rhythm to be clapped, because the rhythm is then felt within a regular metrical framework of strong and weak beats.

Practice exercises

(i) *Listen to this piece, then I'll ask you about ...* [choose one of the first three features listed below the piece] *and about character.* [After playing, ask one question at a time.]

(ii) *Now clap the rhythm of the notes in this phrase, after I've played it twice more.* [Play the extract once.] *Here it is again.* [Repeat the extract.] *... Is it in two time, three time or four time? ... Thank you.*

J. N. Hummel

Dynamics: *What was the general dynamic level of the music, and did this change anywhere?*
Tempo: *Was there any change in tempo, or did it always stay the same?*
Tonality: *Was the music in a major key or in a minor key?*
Character: *What in the music gives this piece its character?*

Gounod

* Omit accel. for clapping.

Articulation: ***Describe the articulation at the beginning of the piece.***
Tempo: ***Did the tempo change or did it always stay the same?***
Tonality: ***Did the music end in a major key or in a minor key?***
Character: ***What in the music gives this piece its character?***

(i) **Listen to this piece, then I'll ask you about …** [choose one of the first three features listed below the piece] **and about character.** [After playing, ask one question at a time.]

(ii) **Now clap the rhythm of the notes in this phrase, after I've played it twice more.** [Play the extract once.] **Here it is again.** [Repeat the extract.] **… Is it in two time, three time or four time? … Thank you.**

* Omit rit. for clapping.

Articulation: **Were the notes at the beginning of the melody mostly smooth or mostly detached?**
Tempo: **Was there any change in tempo, or did it always stay the same?**
Tonality: **Was this piece in a major key or in a minor key?**
Character: **What in the music gives this piece its character?**

Dynamics: **Describe what happened in the dynamics in the second half of the piece, from where the music began quietly.**

Tempo: **Did the tempo change or did it always stay the same?**

Tonality: **Did the music start in a major key or in a minor key?**

Character: **What in the music gives this piece its character?**

(i) *Listen to this piece, then I'll ask you about ...* [choose one of the first three features listed below the piece] *and about character.* [After playing, ask one question at a time.]

(ii) *Now clap the rhythm of the notes in this phrase, after I've played it twice more.* [Play the extract once.] *Here it is again.* [Repeat the extract.] *... Is it in two time, three time or four time? ... Thank you.*

Extract from 'Morris Dance' from *Henry VIII*
© Copyright 1892 Novello & Company Limited for France, Italy, Mexico and Spain
All rights reserved. Used by permission.

Dynamics: *Describe the dynamics in the first half of this piece.*
Articulation: *Were the chords in the accompaniment smooth or detached?*
Tonality: *Did the music end in a major key or in a minor key?*
Character: *What in the music gives this piece its character?*

Dynamics: ***Describe the dynamics in this piece.***

Tempo: ***Was there any change in tempo, or did it always stay the same?***

Tonality: ***Was the music in a major key or in a minor key?***

Character: ***What in the music gives this piece its character?***

Grade 5 aural tests

At a glance

Test 5A | **Melodic repetition**
Sing or play from memory a melody heard twice.

Test 5B | **Sight-singing**
Sing six notes from score in free time.

Test 5C | **(i) Musical features**
Listen to a piece and answer questions about dynamics, articulation, tempo change, tonality or character, and about style and period.

(ii) Rhythmic repetition and metre
Clap the rhythm of a short extract heard twice, and then identify the metre.

Test 5A | Melodic repetition

What the test involves

Syllabus description:

> **To sing or play from memory a melody played twice by the examiner.** The melody will be within the range of an octave, in a major or minor key with up to three sharps or flats. First the examiner will play the key-chord and the starting note and then count in two bars. (If the candidate chooses to play, the examiner will also name the key-chord and the starting note, as appropriate for the instrument.) If necessary, the examiner will play the melody again and allow a second attempt (although this will affect the assessment).

Examiner rubric:

> *Here is a melody for you to repeat. Would you prefer to sing it or play it? ... I'll play it twice. Here is the key-chord* [play] *and your starting note* [play]**.** [Count in two bars, then play the melody once.] *Here it is again.* [Repeat the melody without counting in.] *... Thank you.*

The melody will begin on a note from the tonic triad and will not include any chromatic notes. It will be no more than four bars long in two time (including 6/8), three time or four time.

Many of the melodies include articulation, and all have a dynamic marking. Candidates may reflect the articulation and dynamic in their response if they wish. For the purposes of the exam, however, accuracy of pitch and rhythm are the only elements which the examiner will assess in this test.

For further guidance on responding to this test, see Playing and Singing/humming/whistling on pp. 10–11.

Teaching hints and strategies

The only difference here from Test 4A is the overall complexity of the musical material involved. For those students who find aural repetition difficult, it may be useful to revisit some examples that separate the rhythm from the pitch, such as those found on p. 16.

A good starting point at Grade 5 is to ask your student to sing or play back some simple melodies that combine triadic and scalic patterns in major and minor keys. The following examples use fairly simple rhythms, and start and finish on the tonic. Introduce these examples, and any others that you create yourself, by giving the key-chord and starting note, then counting in two bars. This will help your student place the phrase within its tonal context, and grasp how the rhythm fits with the pulse.

Now you can introduce leaps that involve notes from outside the tonic triad as well. To start with, limit these to 3rds. You could also widen the range to an octave, as in the first of the following examples, and begin on a note from the tonic triad other than the tonic.

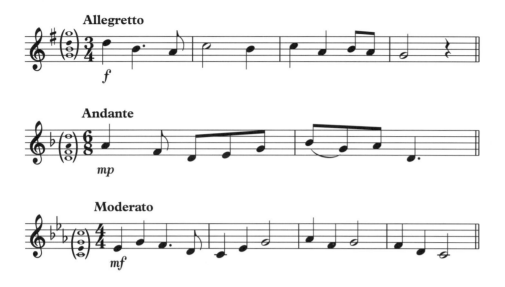

The next stage is to incorporate other intervals, using both their ascending and descending versions. In the first of the examples below, for example, there is a drop of a 5th from the 7th to the 3rd degree of the scale. You could also mix singing back phrases with playing them back, perhaps asking your student to play a phrase once it has been correctly sung. As with Test 4A, the melody may begin with an upbeat, so make the natural rhythmic emphasis clear both in your count-in and in your playing, stressing the first strong beat to help your student make full sense of the melodic shape.

As mentioned at Grade 4, it is worth encouraging your student to sing or play back the melody immediately – almost like one of the echoes in earlier grades. With any delay in response, memory tends to fade and sense of pulse can be lost, often leading to a less certain or reliable outcome than one which is prompt.

Practice exercises

Here is a melody for you to repeat. Would you prefer to sing it or play it?* *... I'll play it twice. Here is the key-chord* [play] *and your starting note* [play]. [Count in two bars, then play the melody once.] *Here it is again.* [Repeat the melody without counting in.] *... Thank you.*

* [If the candidate chooses to play, name as well as play the key-chord and starting note. With transposing instruments use only the examples specified, naming the key-chord and starting note as shown, according to the instrument.]

Minuet — Mozart

Transposing instruments **in B♭**: F major, starting note F; **in F**: B♭ major, starting note B♭; **in E♭**: C major, starting note C

Allegretto — Danish folksong

Transposing instruments **in B♭**: D major, starting note A; **in F**: G major, starting note D; **in E♭**: A major, starting note E

Larghetto — Handel

Transposing instruments **in B♭**: D major, starting note D; **in F**: G major, starting note G; **in E♭**: A major, starting note A

Larghetto — Mozart

Transposing instruments **in B♭**: C major, starting note G; **in F**: F major, starting note C; **in E♭**: G major, starting note D

Allegro — Haydn

Transposing instruments **in B♭**: G major, starting note D; **in F**: C major, starting note G; **in E♭**: D major, starting note A

Allegretto — English tune

Transposing instruments **in B♭**: G major, starting note G; **in F**: C major, starting note C; **in E♭**: D major, starting note D

Allegretto — Diabelli

Transposing instruments **in B♭**: A minor, starting note E; **in F**: D minor, starting note A; **in E♭**: E minor, starting note B

Andante — Schubert

Transposing instruments **in B♭**: D major, starting note A; **in F**: G major, starting note D; **in E♭**: A major, starting note E

Test 5B Sight-singing

What the test involves

Syllabus description:

> **To sing six notes from score in free time.** The candidate may choose to sing from treble or bass clef. The notes will be within the range of a 5th above and a 4th below the tonic, in a major key with up to two sharps or flats. The test will begin and end on the tonic and will not contain intervals greater than a 3rd, except for the rising 4th from dominant to tonic. First the examiner will name and play the key-chord and the starting note. If necessary, the examiner will help the candidate by playing and identifying the correct note if any note is sung at the wrong pitch.

Examiner rubric:

> [When appropriate: *Would you prefer to sing notes in treble clef or bass clef?*] *Please sing the notes at number … on this page. Sing them slowly, and I'll help by giving you the right note if you sing a wrong one. Here is the key-chord* [name and play] *and this is your starting note* [name and play]. *… Thank you.*

A pulse is not given for this test, enabling candidates to choose their speed as well as allowing 'thinking time' between notes, if needed.

For further guidance on responding to this test, see Singing/humming/whistling on pp. 10–11.

Teaching hints and strategies

While intervals in Test 4B do not exceed a 3rd, Test 5B may include the interval of a 4th. This will be a rising dominant to tonic, with its distinctive feeling of closure. To get accustomed to this interval it would first be useful to ensure that your student recognizes what it looks like on the stave. It will always involve line to space or space to line:

This notation then needs to be set in the context of a key, so that your student can not only identify the interval visually but also hear it in his or her head and, more importantly, sing it. Using the examples below, you could begin by playing the key-chord and starting note and then singing the interval for your student to echo while following the notes on the page. Once that is secure, you can then play the key-chord and the dominant note and ask your student to sing the rising 4th interval without help.

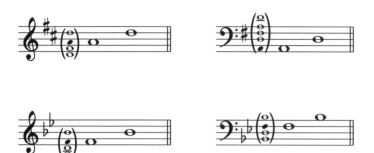

The next step would be to combine the rising 4th interval with 2nds and 3rds (which were covered at Grade 4), always starting with the tonic. Echo work, with your student following the notes, is again a helpful way to begin and to develop confidence before he or she attempts to sight-sing the notes. Build up gradually from four notes to the full six that will be required in the test itself. As mentioned at Grade 4, some teachers will want to incorporate sol-fa names when preparing this with their students, while others might encourage their students to sing the letter names. There are several different ways to approach this, and it is perfectly acceptable in the exam for candidates to vocalize the notes in any way they wish; there is no requirement to sing note names.

4 notes

5 notes

6 notes

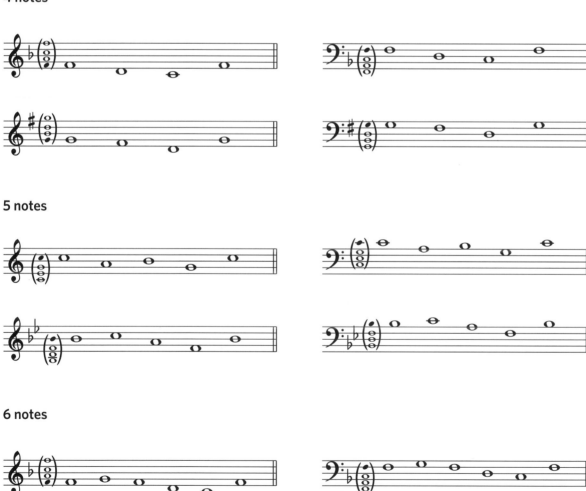

Not all tests will include the rising 4th interval; some may only use a mixture of stepwise movement and 3rds, as shown in the examples below. You may wish to draw your student's attention to where the semitones occur (between mediant and subdominant, and between leading note and tonic).

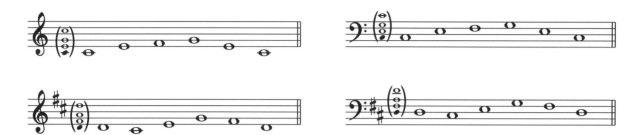

Remember to encourage your students to sing confidently, as a note sung quietly or tentatively will not provide a firm launch-pad from which to aim for the next note. Holding each note for a reasonable length of time – perhaps a couple of seconds – will help to ensure certainty of pitch. (In the exam, this will also enable the examiner to help by playing the right note if the pitching is incorrect.)

Practice exercises

[When appropriate: *Would you prefer to sing notes in treble or bass clef?*] *Please sing the notes at number … on this page. Sing them slowly, and I'll help by giving you the right note if you sing a wrong one. Here is the key-chord* [name and play] *and this is your starting note* [name and play]. *… Thank you.*

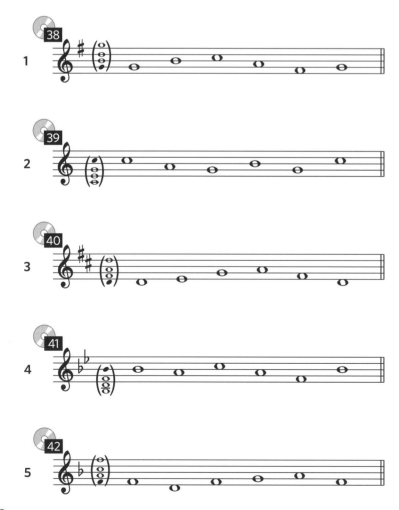

Test 5C (i) Musical features

What the test involves

Syllabus description:

> **To answer questions about two features of a piece played by the examiner.** Before playing, the examiner will tell the candidate which two features the questions will be about. The first will be *one* of the following: dynamics, articulation, tempo, tonality, character; the second will be style and period.

Examiner rubric:

> **Listen to this piece, then I'll ask you about ...** [choose one of the first three features listed below the piece] **and about style and period.** [After playing, ask one question at a time.]

This test builds on questions asked at earlier grades about dynamics, articulation, tempo, tonality and character. In addition, candidates will be asked to identify the style and period of the music (Baroque, Classical, Romantic or 20th century). As with questions on musical character at Grade 4, the candidate needs to identify not only the music's style and period but also the features of the music which point to that conclusion.

The examiner is looking for a ready, confident response that shows perceptive awareness of the relevant musical features.

For further guidance on responding to this part of the test, see Speaking on p. 11.

Teaching hints and strategies

The questions about dynamics, articulation, tempo, tonality and character are very similar to those about the same elements at Grade 4. For any students wishing to revisit these areas, teaching hints and strategies for the character element are given on pp. 24–27 and can be found for the other elements in *Aural Training in Practice*, Grades 1–3, though the questions on these elements are more challenging at Grade 5. For example, candidates might now be asked to describe the dynamics, rather than being asked more specific questions such as whether the first half was louder than the second. Similarly, questions about articulation might now focus on a specific part of the texture, such as accompanying chords or the melodic line.

Answering questions about style and period can be quite difficult for students who have not had varied opportunities for listening to unfamiliar music. However, by Grade 5 your students' stylistic awareness is likely to be emerging as much through their own playing or singing as through their listening activities. As their teacher, you need to draw together your students' musical experiences to help them prepare for this test.

There is no better place to start than with the repertoire your students are learning, and this is an excellent opportunity for aural training to be integrated into your teaching. Discussing the stylistic features of a piece (for which you may find it useful to refer to some of the 'stylistic hallmarks' listed opposite), and exploring how – together – they suggest the period in which it was written, will help to raise musical awareness. As well as helping students to learn about the main periods of music history, it will enhance their interpretative skills as performers. The more they become aware of and understand the characteristics of different styles of music, the more able they will be to project and communicate them in their own playing or singing, thereby giving performances which are more stylistically aware.

Encouraging students to explore music related to the pieces they are learning will further develop their understanding of style and period. As each student will probably be working on at least two or three pieces or songs that come from different periods or are in different styles, you could use these pieces as starting points to create 'listening journeys'. The kinds of questions you might ask your student in order to put together a listening journey include:

- are there other movements from the same work, or perhaps other pieces from the same collection?

- are there different versions of the same work, such as an orchestral or chamber music version?

- what other works can be found by the same composer, or by a contemporary?

- what other works can be found in the same style – minuet, waltz, invention etc.?

Exploring the answers to these kinds of questions will provide ideas for repertoire to form listening journeys. These will prove helpful in preparing for the aural tests while, more importantly, supporting your student's wider musical development. Students should be encouraged to listen to a wide variety of music from different periods, including orchestral, chamber, vocal and solo instrumental music, both live and recorded. The internet provides access to a huge range of audio and video recordings and can be a useful resource here. Since the aural tests in the exam will be played on the piano, it is especially important for students to include keyboard repertoire within their listening.

Stylistic hallmarks

The following stylistic hallmarks given for the music of each period are provided as starting points for discussion with students. They relate to the kinds of piano examples that candidates are likely to hear in a Grade 5 aural test, rather than to each period more generally, and should therefore in no way be considered as exclusive or comprehensive descriptors for any period. These stylistic hallmarks should be considered in combination with each other, as clearly many of them can apply to music of any period. As the grades progress, candidates will be required to identify a wider range of features and more subtle characteristics of each style.

To give some useful starting points for listening activities, four representative composers whose output includes a significant amount of keyboard music have been listed under each period below but, of course, there are all kinds of listening journeys that can be taken!

Baroque

- energetic, lively rhythms, often with an 18th-century dance character
- strong, spirited melodic ideas in both upper and lower parts, sometimes with parts copying each other
- melodic decoration and ornamentation, especially at the end of phrases
- crisp, light articulation with limited pitch and dynamic range, reflecting original use of the harpsichord

Some composers to listen to: J. S. Bach, Handel, D. Scarlatti, Couperin

Classical

- regular, clear-cut phrase lengths that are clearly punctuated (e.g. 4 + 4 bars)
- graceful and elegant melodic ideas, often involving repetition
- accompaniments that clearly outline the generally simple harmony, either with chords or broken-chord patterns (e.g. Alberti bass)
- dynamic shaping, with use of crescendo and diminuendo

Some composers to listen to: Beethoven (early period), Clementi, Haydn, Mozart

Romantic

- flexibility of tempo, including use of rubato
- lyrical and song-like melodies which are not necessarily in the top part, with extended phrases and less obvious punctuation
- rich harmonies and expressive use of chromatic notes
- thicker sonorities, with significant use of the sustaining pedal in piano music, and greater emphasis on a wide dynamic range

Some composers to listen to: Brahms, Chopin, Grieg, Schumann

20th century

- vigorous rhythms, with use of spiky accents and possible use of syncopation and jazz ideas
- freer melodic phrasing, often with unpredictable phrase lengths
- harmony likely to be more adventurous and dissonant, with a variety of chord types
- wide dynamic possibilities, sometimes featuring sudden changes, and use of vivid colours

Some composers to listen to: Bartók, Debussy, Gershwin, Prokofiev

Test 5C   (ii) Rhythmic repetition and metre

What the test involves

Syllabus description:

> **To clap the rhythm of the notes in an extract from the same piece** [as for part (i)]**, and to identify whether it is in two time, three time or four time.** The examiner will play the extract twice (unharmonized), after which the candidate should clap back the rhythm. The examiner will then ask whether the music is in two time, three time or four time. The candidate is *not* required to state the time signature.

Examiner rubric:

> *Now clap the rhythm of the notes in this phrase, after I've played it twice more.* [Play the extract once.] *Here it is again.* [Repeat the extract.] *... Is it in two time, three time or four time? ... Thank you.*

The rhythm to be clapped will be up to approximately six bars in two time or four bars in three or four time. Although a piece may be in 6/8 (the only compound time signature used in Test 5C), the candidate should identify it as being in two time.

For further guidance on responding to this part of the test, see Clapping on p. 10.

Teaching hints and strategies

The teaching hints and strategies provided for this part of the test at Grade 4 (pp. 28–30) are equally applicable here. While at Grade 5 the rhythm to be clapped will be slightly longer and/or more complex than before, the basic principle of the test remains the same. To prepare for the additional challenges at this level, you could begin with some phrases that are relatively straightforward rhythmically but longer than those at Grade 4. If you make up some simple tunes that have repetition built in, with both halves having the same rhythm, then the memory aspect is less daunting and confidence can be established:

If necessary these can be taken one phrase at a time, before putting the two phrases together. Alternatively, you could play each example through three or four times before asking your student to clap it back – rather than twice, as in the exam. The next stage is to alter the rhythm of the second phrase. Here follow a couple of possibilities using the examples above:

As at Grade 4, in the early stages it can be useful to give a count-in. Although this obviously gives away the metre of the music – which students will eventually have to recognize by themselves – it also provides the underlying pulse of the rhythm to be memorized and clapped. This can be particularly important when the rhythm includes longer note values. By keeping the pulse in mind, students can avoid the common tendency to rush the clapping by inadvertently cutting long notes short.

Remember to encourage your students to try to gain an idea of the metre when the whole piece is played during the first part of the test, since it is usually more obvious when heard in context. Having an idea of the metre ahead of the rhythmic repetition test also helps to make musical sense of the rhythm to be clapped, because the rhythm is then felt within a regular metrical framework of strong and weak beats.

Practice exercises

(i) *Listen to this piece, then I'll ask you about ...* [choose one of the first three features listed below the piece] *and about style and period.* [After playing, ask one question at a time.]

(ii) *Now clap the rhythm of the notes in this phrase, after I've played it twice more.* [Play the extract once.] *Here it is again.* [Repeat the extract.] *... Is it in two time, three time or four time? ... Thank you.*

Dynamics: *Describe the dynamics in this piece.*
Tonality: *Was this piece in a major key or in a minor key?*
Character: *What in the music gives this piece its character?*
Style and Period: *Is this a Baroque, Classical or Romantic piece? Which musical features suggest that to you?*

B. Godard

* Play in strict time for clapping.

Dynamics: ***Where were the quietest points in the music?***

Tempo: ***Was there any change in tempo, or did it always stay the same?***

Character: ***What in the music gives this piece its character?***

Style and Period: ***Is the style and period of this piece Baroque, Classical or Romantic? Which features of the music tell you that?***

(i) *Listen to this piece, then I'll ask you about ...* [choose one of the first three features listed below the piece] *and about style and period.* [After playing, ask one question at a time.]

(ii) *Now clap the rhythm of the notes in this phrase, after I've played it twice more.* [Play the extract once.] *Here it is again.* [Repeat the extract.] *... Is it in two time, three time or four time? ... Thank you.*

Bright and rhythmic, in strict time

Michael Jacques

Dynamics: *Describe the dynamics used in this piece.*

Articulation: *Describe the articulation used in this piece.*

Character: *What in the music gives this piece its character?*

Style and Period: *Is the style and period of this piece Classical, Romantic or 20th century? Which musical features tell you that?*

Allegro, ma non troppo

Handel

f (non legato)

* Omit trills for clapping.

Articulation: **Describe the articulation used in this piece.**

Tempo: **Was there any change in tempo, or did it stay the same throughout?**

Character: **What in the music gives this piece its character?**

Style and Period: **Is the style and period of this piece Baroque, Classical or Romantic? Which musical features tell you that?**

(i) *Listen to this piece, then I'll ask you about ...* [choose one of the first three features listed below the piece] *and about style and period.* [After playing, ask one question at a time.]

(ii) *Now clap the rhythm of the notes in this phrase, after I've played it twice more.* [Play the extract once.] *Here it is again.* [Repeat the extract.] *... Is it in two time, three time or four time? ... Thank you.*

Extract from 'Nimrod' from Variations on an Original Theme ('Enigma'), Op. 36

Dynamics: *Describe the dynamics in this piece.*
Tempo: *Was there any change in tempo, or did it always stay the same?*
Character: *What in the music gives this piece its character?*
Style and Period: *Is this piece Baroque, Classical or Romantic in style? Which musical features suggest that to you?*

Tempo: ***Was there any change in tempo, or did it always stay the same?***
Tonality: ***Did this piece end in a major key or in a minor key?***
Character: ***What in the music gives this piece its character?***
Style and Period: ***Is this a Classical, Romantic or 20th-century piece? Which musical features tell you that?***

Answers

Model answers for the practice exercise for Tests 4C(i) and 5C(i) are printed here as a guide to the sort of responses that would be successful in an exam. Full credit would be given to these answers, if given promptly and confidently. However, they are neither definitive nor comprehensive and there are other ways of responding to the questions that would be equally successful. For some questions, candidates would not have to mention all the features given below in order to receive full credit. For example, in answering questions on character or style and period, giving two of the features listed would be sufficient. The supplied answers to questions on character give a list of features followed by two possible adjectives that describe the character of the piece. Candidates may equally well use a different adjective – the important thing is that they identify relevant musical features which support their personal response.

Marks are not awarded for individual tests but reflect the candidate's overall performance during the set of tests as a whole. Candidates are encouraged to use Italian or other musical terms in their answers where appropriate, and this is sometimes shown in the indicative responses below; any clear description is acceptable. The assessment criteria are given on pp. 11–12.

Grade 4

Test 4C(i)

1. J. N. Hummel
   Dynamics: Generally quiet, with crescendo and diminuendo at end of each half
   Tempo: It slowed down towards the end
   Tonality: Major
   Character: Varied articulations, dotted/jumpy rhythms, major key, mainly quiet dynamic; gentle, happy

2. Gounod
   Articulation: Detached
   Tempo: Accelerando towards the end
   Tonality: Minor
   Character: Staccato articulation, dynamic changes, short phrases, accelerando towards the end; playful, cheeky

3. T. Kullak
   Articulation: Detached
   Tempo: It slowed down towards the end
   Tonality: Minor
   Character: Generally quiet dynamic, sudden/surprising f towards the end, detached notes in melody, minor key; mysterious, dramatic

4. Schubert
   Dynamics: Crescendo to f, diminuendo back to p
   Tempo: Rit. towards middle, then back to original tempo
   Tonality: Major
   Character: Slow tempo, smooth melody, gradual dynamic changes; calm, song-like

5. E. German
   Dynamics: Started p then got louder
   Articulation: Detached
   Tonality: Minor
   Character: Fast tempo, staccato chords in the accompaniment, smooth notes in the melody, repeated rhythmic patterns; lively, dance-like

6. Beethoven
   Dynamics: Mainly quiet, with some crescendos and diminuendos
   Tempo: It stayed the same
   Tonality: Minor
   Character: Low register/note range, slow tempo, dotted rhythms, minor key; sad, slow march

Grade 5

Test 5C(i)

1. Mozart
   Dynamics: Each half started quietly and then got louder
   Tonality: Minor
   Character: Dynamic contrasts, scalic runs, variety of
   accompaniment ideas, minor key; dramatic, changeable
   Style and Period: Classical; use of scale and broken chord
   patterns, clearly defined phrases with crescendos,
   repetition of ideas, mainly simple harmony

2. B. Godard
   Dynamics: At the beginning and at the end
   Tempo: It slowed down towards the end
   Character: Moderate tempo, flowing melodic lines, gradual
   and frequent dynamic changes, major key; gentle, calm
   Style and Period: Romantic; flowing melody, use of rubato,
   rich/warm chords, use of the sustaining pedal

3. Michael Jacques
   Dynamics: Mostly loud to very loud, with some abrupt
   changes
   Articulation: A mixture of staccato and legato, with some
   accents towards the end
   Character: Fast tempo, mainly loud dynamic, major chords,
   strong rhythmic feel; energetic, bold
   Style and Period: 20th century; abrupt dynamic changes,
   wide dynamic range, vigorous rhythms, use of unrelated
   chords, percussive sound, dissonant chords near the end

4. Handel
   Articulation: Mainly detached
   Tempo: It stayed the same
   Character: Loud dynamic, triple metre, dotted rhythms,
   major key; lively, dance-like
   Style and Period: Baroque; ornamentation, crisp articulation,
   dance-like style

5. Elgar
   Dynamics: Started very quietly, then crescendo to f in
   middle followed by diminuendo towards the end; it ended
   very quietly
   Tempo: It slowed down in the middle, then back to original
   tempo; rit. at end
   Character: Slow flexible tempo, wide-ranging and smooth
   melody, rich harmony/thick chords; noble, serious
   Style and Period: Romantic; full/sonorous chords, use of the
   sustaining pedal, broad range of dynamics, flexibility of
   tempo, use of a wide range of the keyboard

6. Kabalevsky
   Tempo: It stayed the same
   Tonality: Minor
   Character: Accented chords, loud dynamic, short phrases
   and dissonant/clashing notes; serious, angry
   Style and Period: 20th century; use of a wide range of the
   keyboard, parallel chords, strong accents, dissonant/
   clashing notes

CD track list

Grade 4

Tracks

1–8	Test 4A practice exercises
9–16	Test 4B practice exercises
17–22	Test 4C(i) teaching hints and strategies
23	Test 4C(ii) teaching hints and strategies
24–29	Test 4C practice exercises

Grade 5

Tracks

30–37	Test 5A practice exercises
38–45	Test 5B practice exercises
46–51	Test 5C practice exercises

Key-chords and starting notes for Tests 4A and 5A

For students who choose to play for Test 4A or 5A, key-chords and starting notes are as follows (listed by track number):

Test 4A

1   D minor, starting note D
    in B♭: E minor, starting note E
    in F: A minor, starting note A
    in E♭: B minor, starting note B
2   A major, starting note E
3   D minor, starting note D
    in B♭: E minor, starting note E
    in F: A minor, starting note A
    in E♭: B minor, starting note B
4   F major, starting note C
    in B♭: G major, starting note D
    in F: C major, starting note G
    in E♭: D major, starting note A
5   C minor, starting note C
    in B♭: D minor, starting note D
    in F: G minor, starting note G
    in E♭: A minor, starting note A
6   F major, starting note F
    in B♭: G major, starting note G
    in F: C major, starting note C
    in E♭: D major, starting note D
7   E♭ major, starting note B♭
    in B♭: F major, starting note C
    in F: B♭ major, starting note F
    in E♭: C major, starting note G
8   G major, starting note G
    in B♭: A major, starting note A
    in F: D major, starting note D

Test 5A

30   E♭ major, starting note E♭
    in B♭: F major, starting note F
    in F: B♭ major, starting note B♭
    in E♭: C major, starting note C
31   C major, starting note G
    in B♭: D major, starting note A
    in F: G major, starting note D
    in E♭: A major, starting note E
32   C major, starting note C
    in B♭: D major, starting note D
    in F: G major, starting note G
    in E♭: A major, starting note A
33   B♭ major, starting note F
    in B♭: C major, starting note G
    in F: F major, starting note C
    in E♭: G major, starting note D
34   F major, starting note C
    in B♭: G major, starting note D
    in F: C major, starting note G
    in E♭: D major, starting note A
35   F major, starting note F
    in B♭: G major, starting note G
    in F: C major, starting note C
    in E♭: D major, starting note D
36   G minor, starting note D
    in B♭: A minor, starting note E
    in F: D minor, starting note A
    in E♭: E minor, starting note B
37   C major, starting note G
    in B♭: D major, starting note A
    in F: G major, starting note D
    in E♭: A major, starting note E